Swan Harbor

A NATURE COUNTING BOOK

Laura Rankin

Dial Books for Young Readers  *New York*

For my sister, Beth, with love

Published by Dial Books for Young Readers
A division of Penguin Putnam Inc.
345 Hudson Street
New York, New York 10014

Designed by Nancy R. Leo-Kelly
Text set in Adobe Garamond and Frutiger
Manufactured in China on acid-free paper
1 3 5 7 9 10 8 6 4 2

Library of Congress Cataloging-in-Publication Data
Rankin, Laura.
Swan Harbor : a nature counting book / Laura Rankin.
p.   cm.
ISBN 0-8037-2561-2
1. Counting—Juvenile literature. [1. Counting. 2. Plants. 3. Animals.] I. Title.
QA113 .R36 2003   513.2'11—dc21   00-063862

The artwork was prepared with acrylic inks and paints on Arches watercolor paper.

Welcome to Swan Harbor.

It's similar to so many places along the coast of Maine, my home.
This is a place full of variety and surprise: You never know what you'll see here.
Dragonflies dart by in the spring, and baby robins are born.
Sea roses perfume the air in summer, as ducklings take their first swim.
I've watched hundreds of monarch butterflies dance through the trees in the fall,
and one crisp winter day, I counted sixty-three swans congregating by the shore.

Come take a walk with me.
Count with me the many wonders of nature.
Let me show you Swan Harbor through the seasons.

Swan Harbor

1

robin

2

baby robins

3

squirrels

4

rabbits

5

irises

6

dragonflies

7

water lilies

8

sunfish

9

turtles

10

sea roses

11

ducks

12

seashells

13

cormorants

14

sandpipers

15

starfish

16

lobsters

17

seals

18

butterflies

19

leaves

20

swans

17 seals

18 butterflies

19 leaves

20 swans

1 robin

2 baby robins

3 squirre

5 iri

4 rabbits

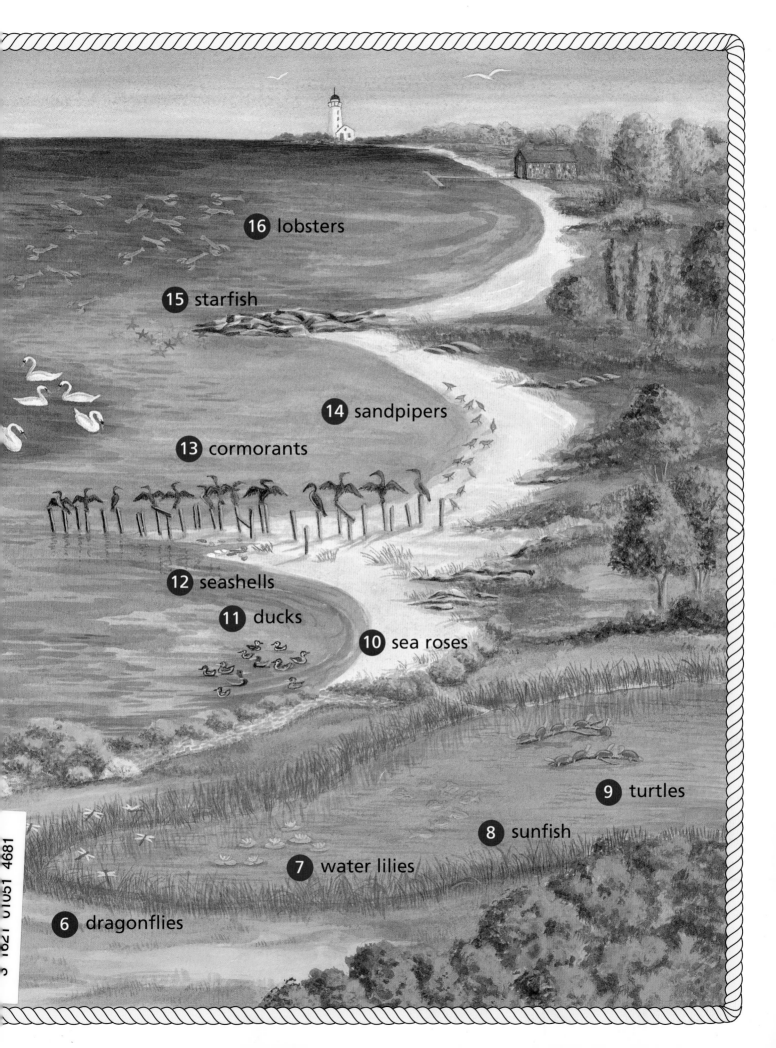

16 lobsters

15 starfish

14 sandpipers

13 cormorants

12 seashells

11 ducks

10 sea roses

9 turtles

8 sunfish

7 water lilies

6 dragonflies

Intriguing Nature Facts

1. American Robins

are a familiar sight throughout North America. In summer, these red-breasted songbirds breed as far north as Canada and Alaska. In autumn, many migrate to warmer locations in the south, flying north again in early spring. You can watch them poke for worms and listen to their lilting song: "Cheer-up cheerily! Cheer-up cheerily!"

2. Baby Robins

are called nestlings or chicks. Robins usually have three to five chicks per nest, or clutch, though only two are shown here. They will be ready to fly about four weeks after they're born. When the baby robins are almost grown, the mother leaves them to begin a second nest of eggs. The father stays behind to care for them until they are ready to be on their own. They will need a full year of life before they mate and have their own families.

3. Eastern Gray Squirrels

have long, bushy tails that help them balance as they leap from branch to branch through the trees. They also use their tails as shelter from the sun, rain, and cold. These busy mammals store nuts and seeds for winter food by burying them in the ground. A squirrel can find its hidden stash under the snow by using its keen sense of smell.

4. Eastern Cottontail Rabbits

live in the shelter of hedges and shrubs. They eat a wide variety of green plants in the summer, and twigs and bark in the winter. Cottontails are mostly active at night, feeding from early evening to the first light of dawn. They usually hop, but can leap as far as ten to fifteen feet.

5. Wild Irises,

or Blue Flags, bloom throughout the northeast from late spring through August. You can see these flowers dotting the shorelines of ponds and marshes or scattered through moist meadows and swampy areas.

6. Dragonflies

live near freshwater streams, ponds, marshes, and lakes. They have specialized wings that allow them to fly both forward *and* backward! Humans benefit from these insects because they eat huge amounts of mosquitoes. The red dragonflies shown in this book are male Half-banded Topers, but dragonflies come in many different varieties.

7. The Fragrant Water Lily

is one of the most common water lilies and can be found throughout North America. The blossoms and leaves float on the surface of the water, growing up on long stems from the muddy bottoms of ponds, lakes, and slow-moving rivers. You can see these flowers from early summer to September.

8. Sunfish

are named for their bright, iridescent coloring. The species shown here are called Pumpkinseeds. These small pond- and lake-dwelling fish are native to the east but have been transplanted to ponds and lakes in many parts of the U.S. They are related to large- and small-mouthed bass.

9. Painted Turtles

live near shallow, weedy freshwater and eat plants, small animals, and insects. These turtles bask together on logs in the sun, but they are wary creatures and will slip quickly into the water if approached. The shell length of a painted turtle is between 4 and 9 3/4 inches.

10. Sea Rose

and Beach Rose are other common names for the Rugosa Rose. This flower grows abundantly in thick hedges, ranging from Quebec, Canada, to New Jersey in the east, and as far west as Minnesota. Along the coast of Maine, its soft fragrance drifts on the sea air from late spring to early fall. After the flower falls away, a round rose hip forms. Rose hips are full of vitamin C and can be used to make tea or jelly.

11. Mallards

are the most common ducks in the Northern Hemisphere, breeding in North America, Europe, and Asia. They eat seeds, grains, insects, and small aquatic animals. The male mallard has a green head with a white ring around its neck. The female is brown-speckled, and thus perfectly camouflaged from predators as she sits on her nest of seven to ten eggs.

12. Seashells

can be found all along the ocean shore and were once the homes of living creatures. Shown in this book, clockwise from lower left, are the shells of: a Surf Clam, a Northern Quahog, a Common Blue Mussel, a Rock Crab, an Atlantic Moonsnail, an Atlantic Bay Scallop, a Sand Dollar, an Atlantic Jackknife Clam, another Common Blue Mussel, a Sea Urchin, a Smooth Periwinkle, and an Atlantic Dogwinkle.

13. Double-crested Cormorants,

or shags, dive and swim expertly under water, catching fish for food. But cormorants do not have natural oils in their feathers to repel water; after swimming, they perch on top of posts or rocks with their wings spread out—like wet laundry!—to dry. Double-crested cormorants are migrating birds that can be found near large bodies of water throughout North America.

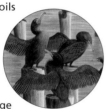

14. Sanderlings

are a type of sandpiper found worldwide on any ocean coast. In the summer, their heads and throats are a dull reddish color. This changes in the winter months to a plumage of soft gray. Sanderlings chatter constantly as they chase the water's edge, eating tiny sea creatures left by the receding tide.

15. Northern Sea Stars,

also called Common Sea Stars, are one of many species of starfish. They range along the east coast of the Atlantic Ocean from Labrador to Cape Hatteras. On the underside of each of their five arms are hundreds of tiny suction cups used to pry open clam and mussel shells, their main source of food.

16. Northern Lobsters

live on the ocean floor. During the day, they hide in rubble crevices or under rocks. They come out at night to feed on fish, crabs, sea urchins, snails, and even other lobsters. Most of the lobsters we see are one to two pounds, but they have been known to weigh as much as forty pounds and can live to be a hundred years old!

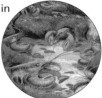

17. Harbor Seals

are in the Hair Seal, or True Seal, family. They have no external ears, and are quite different from Eared Seals, who, with larger front flippers, are more comfortable moving on land. Harbor seals are perfectly adapted to aquatic life, however; they are expert swimmers who can hold their breath under water for up to twenty-seven minutes.

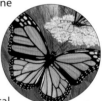

18. Monarch Butterflies

migrate south every autumn and can fly from Maine to Mexico—more than 2,000 miles! They feed on poisonous milkweed plants. There are places along the Maine coast where milkweed grows abundantly; in the fall, monarchs will pause there on their southern flight to feed and rest. For several days, you can see hundreds of butterflies flitting among the weeds and near the ocean shore.

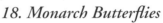

19. Leaves

are filled with chlorophyll that makes them green in the spring and summer. This chlorophyll enables the leaves to make food for the tree. But when the days grow shorter and cooler in the fall, the leaves stop making food and the green fades away to reveal hidden pigments of red or orange or yellow underneath. Then as winter approaches, the leaves dry up and fall to the ground, where they will gradually decay and enrich the soil.

20. Mute Swans

are not really mute: The adults make hissing and grunting noises and the baby swans, called cygnets, make peeping sounds. Swans mate for life, and are extremely protective parents who will fiercely defend their young from any threat, including humans. In the winter, large numbers of mute swans gather together in protected northeastern harbors.